ADF

By Cind

Text Copyright © 2014 Cindy Stringer Wismer

All Rights Reserved

Pearls Publishing House PPH

ISBN-13:978-1499361896

Dedicated to my husband, Michael Wismer.

Table of Contents

Preface:

Introduction

Chapter 1 – ADHD defined

Chapter 2 – Types of ADHD

Chapter 3 – Symptoms

Chapter 4 – Comorbid Conditions

Chapter 5 – Demographics and Causes

Chapter 6 – Interventions and Treatments

Chapter 7 – Assessment and Parent Rights

Chapter 8 – IEP

Chapter 9 – Positives

Conclusion

Preface:

Parenting and/or teaching a child with ADHD requires a wealth of knowledge. I have authored this book in the hope that it will help you in your journey.

While I have used my best efforts in preparing this book, I make no warranties with the respect to the accuracy or completeness of the contents. The advice and strategies contained herein may not be suitable for your situation. You should consult with a professional where appropriate.

Introduction

After teaching for thirty-five years, mostly in the field of special education, I feel compelled to share some of my knowledge with you. Parenting, or teaching, a child with ADHD can be puzzling and over-whelming. Calls from teachers, other people's perception that you aren't parenting well, embarrassing situations, and homework battles are all a part of the ADHD experience. Hopefully this book will lessen some of the confusion and struggles for you and your child.

Included in this book are:

-the definition of ADHD

-types of ADHD

-symptoms of ADHD

-comorbid conditions

-getting your child assessed

-navigating the IEP

-accommodations and modifications

-interventions and treatments

-positives

Chapter 1 – ADHD Defined

Diagnosing a child with ADHD is a multi-step process. Many other conditions such as anxiety, depression and learning disabilities may have some of the same symptoms.

> The American Psychiatric Association's Diagnostic and Statistical Manual, Fifth edition (DSM-5) is used by mental health professionals. Here are the criteria that health-care professionals use. This is for information only. Only professionals can diagnose ADHD.
>
> DSM-5 Criteria for ADHD
>
> People with ADHD show a persistent pattern of inattention and/or hyperactivity-impulsivity that interferes with functioning or development:
>
> 1. Inattention: Six or more symptoms of inattention for children up to age 16, or five or more for adolescents 17 and older; symptoms of inattention have been present for at least 6 months, and they are inappropriate for developmental level:
>   -Often fails to give close attention to details or makes careless mistakes in schoolwork, at work, or with other activities.

-Often has trouble holding attention on tasks or play activities.
-Often does not seem to listen when spoken to directly.
-Often does not follow through on instructions and fails to finish schoolwork, chores, or duties in the workplace (e.g., loses focus, side-tracked).
-Often has trouble organizing tasks and activities.
-Often avoids, dislikes, or is reluctant to do tasks that require mental effort over a long period of time (such as schoolwork or homework).
-Often loses things necessary for tasks and activities (e.g. school materials, pencils, books, tools, wallets, keys, paperwork, eyeglasses, mobile telephones).
-Is easily distracted
-Is often forgetful in daily activities.

2. Hyperactivity and Impulsivity: Six or more symptoms of hyperactivity- impulsivity for children up to age 16, or five or more for adolescents 17 and older and adults; symptoms have been present for at least 6 months to an extent that is disruptive and inappropriate for the person's developmental level:

-Often fidgets with or taps hands or feet, or squirms in seat.

-Often leaves seat in situations when remaining seated is expected.

-Often runs about or climbs in situations where it is not appropriate (adolescents or adults may be limited to feeling restless).

-Often unable to play or take part in leisure activities quietly.

-Is often "on the go' acting as if "driven by a motor."

-Often talks excessively.

-Often blurts out an answer before a question has been completed.

-Often has trouble waiting his/her turn.

-Often interrupts or intrudes on others (e.g., butts into conversations or games)

In addition, the following conditions must be met:

-Several inattentive or hyperactive- impulsive symptoms were present before age 12 years.

-Several symptoms are present in two or more settings (e.g., at home, school or work, with friends or relatives; in other activities).

-There is clear evidence that the symptoms interfere with, or reduce the quality of, social, school, or work functioning.

-The symptoms do not happen only during the course of schizophrenia or another psychotic disorder. The symptoms are not better explained by another mental disorder (e.g., Mood Disorder, Anxiety Disorder, Dissociative Disorder, or a Personality Disorder).

Chapter 2 – Types of ADHD

According to the DSM-5 there are three types of ADHD:

1. Combined presentation
2. Predominantly Inattentive presentation
3. Predominantly Hyperactive- Impulsive presentation

Dr. Amen, a psychiatrist who is the medical director of the Amen Clinics in California, Washington, and Virginia, uses a combination of symptoms and brain scans to identify six types of ADHD:

1. Classic ADHD
2. Inattentive ADHD
3. Over-focused ADHD- ADHD with negative thoughts and behaviors, opposition, arguing
4. Temporal Lobe ADHD- ADHD with irritability, aggressiveness, memory and learning problems
5. Limbic ADHD- ADHD with depression, low energy and decreased motivation
6. The Ring of Fire- ADHD with Bipolar Disorder- moodiness, aggressiveness and anger

Dr. Amen has studied the effects of medication on each type. He has found that different types of ADHD respond better to different medications. In my years as a teacher I observed children on medication. Parents would often try several before finding the medication that benefitted their child.

A note about the Over Focused ADHD. I have often heard comments such as, "My child can't have ADHD. He plays video games for hours." Or teachers say, "He can watch a video, why can't he focus on his work?" Children with this type of ADHD have to ability to hyper-focus on one activity to the exclusion of everything else. They will often get irritated if you try to get their attention.

Chapter 3 – Symptoms

Most children have times of being hyperactive and impulsive. It is normal for preschoolers to have short attention spans. Young children are naturally very active and energetic. However, a child who does not have ADHD will not appear hyperactive, unfocused and impulsive in all settings. They may have problems at home but be able to focus at school.

I found that children with ADHD have difficulty at home, at school and in social situations. When teaching I would see children with ADHD not able to focus even when performing on stage in a program.

If you have ever had Restless Leg Syndrome or an itch that you just had to scratch then you know how difficult it is to not act on those urges.

Symptoms of ADHD may include:

-Difficulty paying attention

-Frequently daydreaming

-Difficulty following through on instructions

-Appearing not to be listening

-Problems with organization

- Forgetfulness
- Losing items such as books, toys, pencils
- Failure to finish homework or chores
- Easily distracted
- Fidgets
- Squirms
- Difficulty remaining seated
- In constant motion
- Excessively talkative
- Interrupts conversations
- Difficulty taking turn

Chapter 4 – Comorbid Conditions

A *comorbid condition* is one or more conditions present in addition to the primary diagnosis- in this case, ADHD.

ADHD is associated with abnormalities in the frontal lobes. Therefore a child with ADHD has increased risk for any neurological condition that originates in these regions. According to the CDC experts feel that comorbidity is not being properly diagnosed. Comorbid conditions often go untreated.

ADHD comorbid conditions:

-Autism- The Journal of Pediatrics states that 20% of children with ADHD have some autistic traits. Consumer health states that children with ADHD are 20 times more likely to have autistic traits such as slow language development, difficulties in interactions and problems with emotional control.

-Bipolar Disorder- Between 16%- 24% of children with ADHD also have Bipolar disorder. The manic phase of bipolar is very similar to the hyperactivity of ADHD.

-Depression-Between 15%-20% of children with ADHD also suffer from depression. It is believed that younger children begin with anxiety which turns to depression as they get older. Symptoms are little tolerance for frustration, not being patient, easily becoming upset.

-Anxiety- Between 25%-33% of children with ADHD also have anxiety. The anxiety may be genetic or may be triggered from unhappiness at school, especially if the child has poor social skills.

-Conduct Disorder (CD)- Between 22% of boys and 8% of girls with ADHD also have a conduct disorder. Symptoms are difficulty following rules or behaving in an acceptable way. The children are sometimes thought of as being "bad" by other students instead of as having a mental illness.

-Oppositional Defiance Disorder (ODD)- Between 35%-50% of children with ADHD also have ODD. ODD symptoms are defiance, extreme stubbornness and anger problems. ODD is more prevalent in boys than girls.

-Learning Disorders (LD)- Between 40%-60% of children with ADHD have learning disorders. Young children who are bright may be able to compensate. As the academic curriculum becomes more difficult the learning disorder is more noticeable. The learning disorder may be a result of inattention or it may be a learning disability such as dyslexia.

-Tourette's Disorder- Children with Tourette's often have ADHD and OCD, a triple disorder. A child may come in for tics and the psychologist finds that the child also has intrusive thoughts of OCD and inattentiveness of ADHD. Doctors at John's Hopkins also found that this combination sometimes fades with adolescence. As the brain develops one or all three may disappear.

-Dysgraphia- Many children with ADHD have difficulty writing legibly. They may be skilled artistically but have difficulty with the conversion of symbolic information. The problem seems to lie in connecting the input of the muscles to the brain. Imagine if you had to 'draw' each letter you wrote. Remediation is often futile in younger children. Teaching keyboarding, using computers or tape recorders are often more effective. However, the good news is, that I saw many children struggle with handwriting as young children and later master it. Printing is easier to learn than cursive for someone with dysgraphia.

-Epilepsy- The connection of ADHD and epilepsy is described by the Cleveland Clinic as a two-way street. Children with epilepsy often have ADHD, with the ADHD symptoms apparent before the first seizure.

-Asthma- According to Consumer Health boys with ADHD are 40% more likely to have asthma and 50% more likely to have allergies.

Chapter 5 – Demographics and Causes

The amount of children diagnosed with ADHD has increased from 7.8% in 2003 to 11% in 2013. Boys are more likely to be diagnosed with 13.2% compared to girls at 5.6%. The average age of diagnosis is seven years. ADHD varies greatly by state with Nevada having the lowest percentage at 5.6% and Kentucky having the highest at 18.7%.

We do not know with certainty what causes ADHD. Experts believe there is a strong genetic component. They believe the levels of certain neurotransmitters in the brain differ in people with ADHD. ADHD tends to run in families. If one parent has ADHD there is a 33% likelihood of their child also having ADHD. It occurs in people of every level of intelligence.

In some cases there is no genetic component. ADHD may be caused by:

-smoking and/or drinking while pregnant

-low birth weight

-head injury, especially to the frontal lobe

-exposure to lead, pesticides, or other environmental toxins

ADHD always begins in childhood with 30%-70% of children still having symptoms as an adult.

Chapter 6 – Interventions and Treatments

Medication is often used to treat ADHD. This is a controversial subject, with some people saying they would never put their child on medication and others saying that ADHD is a medical condition that should be treated.

I taught many children with ADHD. Some responded amazingly well to medication.

I remember one girl (Ann), in particular, whose mother is a nurse. I saw in Ann's IEP that she had ADHD. However, I saw no indication in her behavior. She was able to focus, she was not fidgety and she played well with her friends. One morning, several months into the school year, Ann's behavior was totally different. She wasn't able to stay in her seat, she argued with me and crawled under her desk. I called her mother and found out she had not taken her medication that morning. Her mother came to the school and gave the medication to her. Ann told me she felt better when she takes her medicine. For this little girl medication helped her control her behavior enabling her to function better in the classroom and with friends.

Another student (Luke) started in my class without medication. His mother frequently volunteered. Luke was one of the most hyperactive and aggressive children I taught in my thirty-five years. He would literally throw his desk and books to the floor. Luke would become so frustrated from his inability to write that he would tear his paper and start crying. He wanted to do the work but just couldn't. His mother decided to try medication. It took trying several different medications until they found the right one for Luke. After medication Luke was able to focus and control his anger and aggressiveness. Luke made friends and became a class favorite, always ready with a 'what if' joke to entertain us.

Some students did not respond well to medication.

One boy (Chris) was on several medications. No matter what they tried he was not able to focus and remained hyperactive. Some of the medications would cause him to have tremors and cry.

Another girl (Jane) had a similar experience. Her mother worked closely with the doctor but they were not able to help Jane focus. In fact, after noticing tics, I asked the mother if she would try taking her off the medication. Jane was happier, though still very active, not taking medication.

If you do decide to use medication it is very important to have a teacher who is willing to work closely with you. A teacher should NEVER tell you to put your child on medication. (In fact, I probably over-stepped asking Jane's mother to try no medication.) The parent gives a child his medicine and sends him to school. The teacher will see him more than you during the day and should report back to you her observations.

Stimulant medication is often prescribed for ADHD. It may sound counter-intuitive that a stimulant would be prescribed for hyperactivity. Stimulants are thought to activate the brain circuits reducing hyperactivity. In simple terms, if the brain is active the body is less active. Stimulants also reduce impulsivity and may improve coordination.

There are side effects to stimulants. A decreased appetite and sleep problems are fairly common. Less common are tics.

Whether or not you use medication for your child is your decision. I am not advocating either way.

Behavioral Interventions:

-Structure your child's routine- Children with ADHD function much better with a structured routine. From wake-up to bedtime try to maintain the same schedule. I found a visual schedule helped the child to know what to expect.

-Organization- Try labeling with pictures your child's toy bins and limiting the amount of toys he has in his room. This will make keeping his room clean and organized easier. Store unused toys out of sight. Keep school-age children's backpacks and school work in the same place.

-Limit your directions. When giving directions, make them short and clear.

-Limit choices- Give her/him two choices only. Making decisions is difficult and your child may become over-whelmed with too many choices.

-Homework- Turn off the TV and music! Limit any distractions. Provide a quiet spot for homework. I never played background music in my class- it is too distracting for children.

-Goals and Rewards- It sounds so simple, yet this is probably one of the most effective tools you can use. Sit down with your child and set one goal at a time, e.g. complete my homework, brush my teeth, clean my room. Let them help in deciding what they needs to work on. If it is their goal they 'own' it. Hang the goal sheet on the refrigerator or keep a goal folder where she/he can check it regularly. I used dot-to-dot pictures. After a number of successful days reward your child with something. For younger children you might reward for each day, for older children more days. The reward doesn't need to be something big. It may be a sticker, playing a game with you, going to the park, an ice cream. In my class one of the favorite rewards was 'teacher's chair for the day.' When she/he completes the whole chart a bigger prize (I gave medals, reward ceremony and all), and then set a new goal. Truthfully, your praise at their achievements is probably more important than the prize.

-Make discipline appropriate- No spanking or yelling. No spanking or yelling. We can't 'control' others but we can control our reactions. When chaos erupted in my class I would whisper. Soon the room would get quiet so they could hear me. Some times that didn't work and I would put on music and start dancing. My point is that discipline is to *teach* the child, not to *punish* the child. Approach it with a calm voice of reason. When a child is yelling it only escalates the behavior if you yell back. A short time-out to enable the child to calm down, an apology, a hug and forget about it. Start over. Let her/him know that past discretions are gone.

-Praise- Children thrive with praise. They need your approval. Make sure you give more praise than reprimands. It might be something simple like, "I like how you put your plate in the sink," or "Great job playing nicely." Make an effort to 'catch them being good.' Praise them once for something and they are much more likely to continue the good behavior.

-Success- Just imagine what being ADHD can do to a child's self-esteem. They don't understand why other children are able to sit still and get positive feedback when it is so difficult for them. Find something your child excels at. Jane's mother asked my advice in this area. I first advised Karate, which helps kids focus. That didn't last long. Next I recommended dance (Jane was my star in our programs at school). She had trouble staying focused. Next I gave Jane my son's old violin and we put her in the school orchestra. That was her gift! She is now in High School and still playing. Individual sports seem to work better than team sports. I have read that Ping Pong is very good for improving focus. Succeeding gives your child self-confidence and boosts her/his self-esteem.

-Social Skills- Children with ADHD are often not socially aware. They don't realize that their behavior is inappropriate and really don't know how to interact socially with others. Often they feel alone and isolated from their peers because of their inappropriate behaviors. Skills that come naturally for others need to be taught to children with ADHD. The ideal would be a Social Skills Group specifically designed for children with ADHD. Unfortunately, these are difficult to find. In my class I focused heavily on social skills training. However, in general education the focus nationwide is now on testing. Role-playing is a fun way to teach social skills to little children. You might also look for computer games or videos on this subject.

Social Skills to teach:

*taking turns and sharing- Impatience makes it difficult to wait her/his turn. Role play taking turns. I would make this fun and act silly with the children. Show her/him both the correct way and the wrong way. Be sure to end with the correct way. An example of this - perhaps your child has a friend over and is playing video games. The friend asks how to play. Your child has a tendency to grab the controller and play for him rather than show him how. Of course, your child will say, "I'm showing him how," as a justification for monopolizing the game.

*reciprocal conversation- Is your child overly talkative? Does he/she talk nonstop? Most kids with ADHD are and do. Practice taking turns talking with emphasis on listening to the other person. I used a timer for this so each child had the same amount of time to talk. After each had a turn I would have the child tell me what his friend said.

*personal space- I used to tell the children to pretend like people have a bubble around them. "Don't pop my bubble," was said often in my classroom.

*tone of voice- Sometimes children will talk too loudly. You can use visual cues for this. Mine was a paper radio with a dial. Each student made their own and we had fun 'turning up the volume' and shouting, then 'turning down' the volume to a whisper. I just had to hold up the radio and turn it down to remind them.

*resolving conflicts and cooperation- It is difficult for any child to realize they are not the center of the universe and can't have everything their way. Role-playing is effective in teaching children how to compromise and work together.

Chapter 7 – Assessment and Parent Rights

Early identification and intervention are pivotal in your child's future development. The IDEA (Individuals with Disabilities Education Act), a federal legislation, authorizes states to implement services for infants and toddlers with disabilities. It should be of no cost to the parent. Once your child is in public school it may take years to get your child identified to receive the services to which they are entitled. By identifying your child before Kindergarten you will be ensuring that he/she already has an IEP or 504 in place and the public school will be legally bound to provide services. Having an IEP or 504 does not mean that your child *must* be in a special class. Rather, it ensures that he/she will receive the accommodations necessary to be successful in school.

The first step when you suspect your child has ADHD is getting an assessment. Some parents are successful using their pediatrician and getting a referral to a psychiatrist which is paid for through insurance. However, I have heard many parents say their pediatrician doesn't take them seriously. You know your child much better than your pediatrician who may spend ten minutes with her/him. You can go to the County Superintendent of School's office, your local SELPA (Special Education Local Plan Area) office, or the local school district's special services office and give a written request for testing. They have sixty days to assess.

An IEP meeting will be held to discuss the assessment results and write an IEP (Individualized Education Program). This is a document personalized to your child's educational needs. I will discuss this more in Chapter 8.

Parent Rights vary little from state to state. I recommend you go to your state's Department of Education website to become familiar with these. In California you have the right:

-to participate in any decision regarding your child's educational placement

-TO REFER YOUR CHILD FOR ASSESSMENT! Many states are now using the RTI (response to intervention) method to track children's progress in the general education classroom, delaying referrals to the school psychologist. RTI is the general education teacher trying interventions in the classroom first before referral. RTI requires the teacher to keep a notebook on your child and list what methods she has tried and the results. (e.g. preferential seating, peer tutoring). It sounds like a good idea. Perhaps it's working in some cases. But, in my experiences in CA, in over- crowded classrooms adding more work for the general education teacher is very difficult and those notebooks end up being passed from grade to grade with the child rarely being assessed. AT ANY TIME DURING RTI YOU MAY REQUEST AND ARE ENTITLED TO AN ASSESSMENT for your child. As a teacher I saw many general education teachers frustrated with this system and the delay it caused in getting children referred for testing. The teacher's hands are tied. Many arguments broke out at teachers' meetings between school psychologists and teachers over this issue. The teacher isn't allowed to tell you that you can go to the district office special services and request assessment. Don't let the school psychologist intimidate you. Know your rights. If the district still refuses to assess your child you are entitled to a due process hearing to address this issue.

-to be included in the development of the IEP. You are part of the IEP team. Sometimes school psychologists will come to a meeting having already decided what they are going to offer your child. Come prepared with an idea of what is acceptable to you. You may also bring an advocate, relative or expert with you.

-to written notice of any change in your child's educational program.

-to an Independent Educational Assessment. If you disagree with the psychologist's assessment you have the right to another assessment administered by an impartial person. (Note- I have *rarely* seen a school psychologist make an initial diagnosis of ADHD or Autism- perhaps five in my thirty-five years of teaching. Having your child assessed before beginning Kindergarten and keeping a file with all the information ensures early intervention. In my experiences the district refrains from identifying special needs. In my opinion this is to save money.)

-to have your child 'stay put.' If there is a disagreement in the IEP meeting (e.g. the psychologist wants to move your child to a different class and you don't feel it is best for your child) you have the right for your child to 'stay put' in their present placement until the disagreement is resolved.

-to a hearing regarding any disagreement between you and the school district regarding your child's FAPE (free appropriate public education).

Chapter 8 – IEP

An IEP (Individualized Education Program) is a written document developed for each child who is eligible for special education. It is reviewed and revised at least once a year. IEP's contain pertinent information about your child's educational program.

The IEP will list what services your child receives. Some services are: Language and Speech, Occupational Therapy, Physical Therapy, Adaptive P.E., and counseling. It will name where these services are given: a self-contained special education class, mainstreaming, or services in a learning lab for a part of the day. Most children with ADHD are placed in the general education class perhaps being pulled out of class for a small portion of the day for services.

Accommodations and modifications are listed on the IEP. These, after deciding placement, are the most important part of the IEP. Accommodations and modifications are based on student need and decided by the IEP team. Accommodations refer to adaptations to help the student learn the same curriculum as their peers. Modifications refer to a change in either what is being taught or what is expected from your child.

Some appropriate accommodations for a child with ADHD:

-Seat student near the teacher.

-Seat student near a positive role model.

-Stand near the student when giving directions or presenting lessons.

-Block out distracting stimuli.

-Allow additional time.

-Taped books

-Study Carrel

-Visual aids

-Teach through a multi-sensory approach (visual, auditory, kinesthetic).

-Shorter assignments.

-Reduce homework! After a long day at school children with ADHD should not have to go home to an hour's worth of homework. Studies show homework does not improve outcomes and puts undue stress on family life.

-Use of keyboard. This is especially important if your child has difficulty with handwriting, which many with ADHD do. An Occupational Therapy (OT) pull-out program to teach key boarding skills and access to a computer in the class will lessen the stress of written assignments.

-Shorten spelling tests.

-Communicate daily with parents. I had daily sheets to send home with the student.

-Reversals and transpositions of letters and numbers not marked wrong.

-Highlight main idea in text book. Even when I taught general education I had one or two textbooks that I had highlighted the main ideas of each chapter.

Some appropriate modifications for children with ADHD are:

-Change of curriculum to meet child's academic level

-Student involved in same curriculum with different expectations (e.g. draw picture instead of write paper; or outline instead of essay).

-Use of a calculator for math

-Less homework

-Lower performance goals

Another change you may want is not to have your child participate in state testing. This is something that teachers aren't allowed to tell you, but you may easily opt out of testing by simply putting it in writing. State testing is stressful and demands focusing for a long period of time. Your child is tested annually for her/his IEP. That and his work samples are sufficient to chart his growth.

If you feel your child's teacher is not the right fit request to have him/her moved to another. Some teachers are more experienced, knowledgeable and kinder than others. Occasionally observe your child's teacher and how she relates to your child.

Chapter 9 – Positives

Though ADHD is a serious disorder it does have some positive aspects. People with ADHD tend to look beyond the norm. Impulsive behavior may allow them to try new things without trepidation. ADHD does not slow down the learning process if teachers implement effective teaching strategies geared specifically towards the ADHD learner.

Successful people with ADHD:

Sir Richard Branson

Jim Carrey

Woody Harrelson

Howie Mandel

Pete Rose

Michael Phelps

Robin Williams

Will Smith

The list goes on and on.

Conclusion

I sincerely hope this book has been helpful to parents and teachers alike. With the right strategies and teamwork between home and school your child **will** be successful. Though each day may be a challenge, always be patient and kind.

Please take a few minutes to give this book a review on Amazon and visit me on Facebook @ *Cindy Stringer Wismer author* and *Never Push and Never Pull....a short story.* You can also find me on Twitter and Goodreads.

Sources:

Pediatric Journal

WebMD

Mayo Clinic

John's Hopkins

CDC

Cleveland Clinic

Consumer Health Guide for Parents

Other books by Cindy Stringer Wismer:

Never Push and Never Pull...a short story

A Guide for Parents and Teachers

Stars in the Sand, book#1 of 'the sands series'

The Magic Sands, book#2 of 'the sands series'

ADHD in Adults

Printed in Great Britain
by Amazon